W9-BYA-318

DIVERSITY AND ENTERTAINMENT
Black Lives in Media

Amanda Jackson Green

Lerner Publications ◆ Minneapolis

Content consultant: Dr. Artika R. Tyner, President and CEO of Planting People
Growing Justice

Lerner Publications Company
An imprint of Lerner Publishing Group, Inc.
241 First Avenue North
Minneapolis, MN 55401 USA

For reading levels and more information, look up this title at www.lernerbooks.com.

Library of Congress Cataloging-in-Publication Data

The Cataloging-in-Publication Data for *Diversity and Entertainment: Black Lives in Media* is on
    file at the Library of Congress.
ISBN 978-1-72842-959-5 (lib. bdg.)
ISBN 978-1-72842-027-0 (pbk.)
ISBN 978-1-72842-961-8 (eb pdf)

Manufactured in the United States of America
1 – CG – 12/31/20

Table of Contents

CHAPTER 1

The Silver Screen 4

CHAPTER 2

A Hurtful Past 10

CHAPTER 3

Growing Voices 16

CHAPTER 4

Reclaiming Black Stories 22

Major Moments in Black Media 28

Glossary 30
Learn More 31
Index 32

THE SILVER
Screen

It is February 21, 2018. A group of children fills a movie theater in Atlanta, Georgia. Many of them wear clothing with brightly colored patterns. Some wear kente cloth, the traditional cloth of Ghana, to show their heritage.

The children are watching *Black Panther*. The film is set in the fictional African nation of Wakanda. It is the first major superhero movie with a mostly Black cast. T'Challa, the Black Panther, is the film's protagonist. The movie also features many other Black heroes. This includes T'Challa's sister, Shuri. Shuri uses her smarts to build weapons that protect her brother and other warriors who defend Wakanda. After the movie, one of the girls says she was excited to see so many heroes who looked like her.

Black Panther, starring the late Chadwick Boseman, appealed to audiences of all ages because it dealt with important themes such as race and identity while providing an action-packed superhero story.

INTO THE SPIDER-VERSE

The Amazing Spider-Man is a famous comic book series created by Stan Lee in 1962. The story's main character is Peter Parker, a white boy from New York City. Spider-Man became popular among young superhero fans. One reason was his costume. It fully covered his face and skin. Readers of all skin colors could imagine themselves under the hero's mask.

Spider-Man is one of Marvel's most popular heroes. Since 2002, the character has been the main subject of nine major movies.

For their work on *Spider-Man: Into the Spider-Verse*, Jake Johnson *(left, voice of Peter Parker)* and Shameik Moore *(right, voice of Miles Morales)* attended the Academy Awards in 2019.

The Amazing Spider-Man introduced a new Spider-Man in 2011. He is a biracial teenager from Brooklyn named Miles Morales. His father is Black, and his mother is Latina. His family speaks both English and Spanish at home. He is smart, kind, and funny. For many fans, this new Spider-Man reflected their own lives.

In 2018, Miles was the main character in the film *Spider-Man: Into the Spider-Verse*. It was the first Spider-Man film to reimagine the hero. It was a chance for people of color to see a movie superhero who looked like them.

TELLING A NEW STORY

Movies and TV shows often present negative images of people of color. They are portrayed in ways that limit their strengths, abilities, and achievements. T'Challa and Miles Morales reflect a push for media that challenges these images. Both characters present positive, heroic images of Black people.

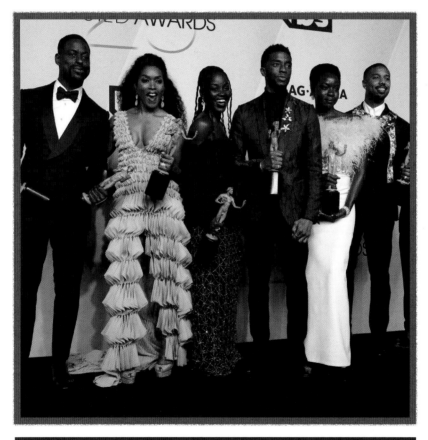

Several African countries inspired the setting, costumes, and language used in *Black Panther*, and many of the actors brought touches from their own cultural backgrounds to their characters.

John Boyega portrayed FN-2817, or Finn, a Stormtrooper who becomes a hero, in three Star Wars films, including *The Rise of Skywalker* in 2019.

Spider-Man: Into the Spider-Verse uses a familiar story to connect with a more diverse audience. But some viewers have resisted changes to well-known stories. In 2015, the movie *Star Wars: The Force Awakens* came out in theaters. It was the first film in the Star Wars series to include a Black actor as a Stormtrooper. Some fans were angry. They said the character was unrealistic because the original Stormtroopers were clones of a white person.

The movie's director, JJ Abrams, pointed to the fact that Stormtroopers existed in a made-up world. He said it is important for people of color to see themselves represented in films.

 We often admire superheroes. What are some traits that you connect to superheroes?

CHAPTER 2

A HURTFUL
Past

The first Black people in America were enslaved. Many were taken from their homes in countries now known as Senegal, the Gambia, Angola, and the Democratic Republic of Congo. They came from different groups, each with its own unique culture. They had distinct languages, clothing styles, music, and dance.

Black people from many cultures were enslaved together. Music was one way they connected. They used scrap materials to recreate familiar instruments such as drums, banjos, and panpipes. They often made up songs while they worked. Over time, their music changed into new styles. This included gospel and blues music.

In the 1930s, radio became popular. Black musicians were rarely given recording contracts. White artists used traditionally Black music styles without giving credit to Black artists. This is an example of cultural appropriation.

Huddie Ledbetter, known on stage as Lead Belly, was called the "King of the 12-String Guitar." His music influenced artists such as the Beatles and the Rolling Stones.

BLACKFACE AND STEREOTYPES

Traveling musicals called minstrelsy were popular in the 1800s. White actors painted their faces black and mocked Black people. This practice is called blackface.

G.H. Elliot was a well-known white entertainer in the United States and Great Britain who was famous for performing in blackface.

Minstrel shows relied on stereotypes. Stereotypes oversimplify and apply traits to everyone in a certain group. They ignore the fact that each person is unique. For example, Black characters in minstrel shows had very dark skin and oversized lips. They were portrayed as unintelligent, lazy, and dishonest.

The Godmother of Rock 'n' Roll

Much of America's popular music is based on the music created by Black enslaved people. A Black woman named Sister Rosetta Tharpe is often credited with inventing the popular 1950s "rock 'n' roll" genre. Tharpe combined forms of Black music to create her own style. This included jazz, blues, and gospel. Many famous singers, like Elvis Presley, were inspired by Tharpe's distinct sound.

NO DIVERSITY ON SCREEN

The first movies were made in the late 1800s. Directors cast only white actors in the films. White actors played Black characters, just as they had in minstrel shows. Blackface and stereotypes remained popular in entertainment.

Black actors got their first movie roles in the 1930s. The roles were usually background parts. White filmmakers believed viewers would not pay to watch Black people in main roles. Sometimes they sang and danced as entertainment for white characters in films.

Paul Robeson first worked as a lawyer. Due to racism in the profession, he decided to become an actor and singer instead. He used music to promote Black culture and civil rights.

Amos 'n' Andy was originally a radio show in which Black characters were voiced by white actors. When the show was adapted for television, Black actors portrayed all of the Black characters.

Television became popular in the 1950s. Between 1955 and 1986, only 6 percent of TV characters were Black. Some TV shows wanted to get more Black viewers. They created small roles for people of color to make casts appear more diverse. This kind of character is called a token minority. Some TV shows continue to use tokenism to attract a larger audience.

 Traditions, stories, and songs can help groups of people feel connected. Do you have any traditions that are important to your family?

CHAPTER 3

GROWING
Voices

In the 1970s, movie studios believed they could make more money by appealing to Black audiences. They began to make films with mainly Black actors. In that decade, studios made more than two hundred movies with mostly Black characters.

The movies featured Black heroes who controlled their own lives. The new films were very popular. Some people believed it was a step toward more Black representation in film.

Others felt the movies exploited, or took advantage of, Black audiences. They thought the films created negative stereotypes of Black people. Many of the films' protagonists were involved in violence and crime. For example, in the popular movie *Super Fly*, the main character sold drugs. A member of the National Association for the Advancement of Colored People (NAACP) named Junius Griffin invented a term for these types of movies: Blaxploitation films.

Super Fly, starring Ron O'Neal, was the first Black-centered movie to be shot entirely by a Black crew.

While humorous and entertaining, *Good Times* also dealt with serious issues such as gang violence, poverty, and discrimination in the Black community.

MORE BALANCED REPRESENTATION

One of the first TV shows to feature a Black family was *Good Times*. It aired in 1974. The show's creator was a white man named Norman Lear. Lear wanted the show to reflect life in a typical Black American home. He consulted Black writers and actors. They based the show on their own experiences.

Good Times became very popular. Fans said it was relatable. The Evans family was similar to their own families. Audiences liked the show because it presented a balanced image of Black people. The characters had strengths as well as flaws. They celebrated and struggled. They were not limited to stereotypes.

In 1984, *The Cosby Show* debuted. The Cosbys were a wealthy Black family from New York. It was the first show to include Black parents with college degrees. The characters were smart, funny, and educated. *The Cosby Show* was popular with audiences worldwide. It was the most-watched show in America for four straight seasons.

Disney Learns by Listening

Disney's 2013 movie *Frozen* included a style of music called joik. Joik is a cultural tradition of the Sami, an Indigenous group in the Nordic region. However, no Sami people were included in the movie. Some Sami people felt that Disney had disrespected their culture.

In 2019, Disney released *Frozen II*. The film included Indigenous characters. The company accepted advice from Sami people about how to portray their music, clothing, and customs. One of the Sami members, Anne Lájla Utsi, said the partnership was a good example of how companies can tell cultural stories with respect.

BLACK ENTERTAINMENT TELEVISION

The success of *Good Times* and *The Cosby Show* proved that viewers enjoyed shows with Black characters. More popular Black sitcoms debuted in the 1990s. This included *The Fresh Prince of Bel-Air* and *Moesha*.

In 1980, a businessman named Robert L. Johnson launched a TV channel just for Black stories. He called the company Black Entertainment Television, or BET. The channel focused on music, TV shows, and movies made by Black artists. BET depicted a wide range of Black stories.

Johnson speaks onstage at an event celebrating twenty-five years of Black Entertainment Television.

In 2002, Halle Berry became the first Black woman to win Best Actress at the Academy Awards.

In the 1990s, Black shows and movies continued to gain popularity. However, Black artists were often left out of popular awards shows. The first Academy Awards were held in 1929. Sidney Poitier became the first Black person to win Best Actor in 1964. By 1999, only six Black actors had won an Oscar. In 2001, BET created the BET Awards. The awards show honors the achievements of people of color in various areas. This includes music, TV, film, sports, and community service. Johnson sold BET for $3 billion in 2001. He became the first Black American billionaire.

Good Times and *The Cosby Show* were among the first shows to feature Black families. What are some of your favorite shows that include people of color? How are they portrayed?

RECLAIMING BLACK
Stories

Several artists have pushed for more Black representation in media. In the early 2000s, Tyler Perry wrote, directed, and acted in his own stage plays. The main character, Madea, was based on Perry's mother and aunt. In the mid-2000s, the plays were adapted into movies. The films made more than $500 million. In 2006, he created Tyler Perry Studios. It is the first major film studio under Black ownership.

In 2010, Black filmmaker Ava DuVernay founded ARRAY. The organization focuses on increasing awareness of films made by women and people of color. Many of DuVernay's own projects are based on actual events in Black history. Her 2019 film, *When They See Us*, tells the story of five Black boys who were imprisoned in 1989 for a crime they did not commit.

According to Tyler Perry, the Madea character was not only a tribute to his aunt and mother, but also a message to the world that Black women are powerful and amazing.

CONFRONTING BIAS

In 2020, a man named George Floyd was killed by police in Minneapolis. His death brought increased attention to the issue of police brutality. This is when police officers use too much force and harm others. Studies showed Black people were at least twice as likely to be victims of police brutality. Many believe this is because of racial bias and stereotypes of Black people as criminals in the media.

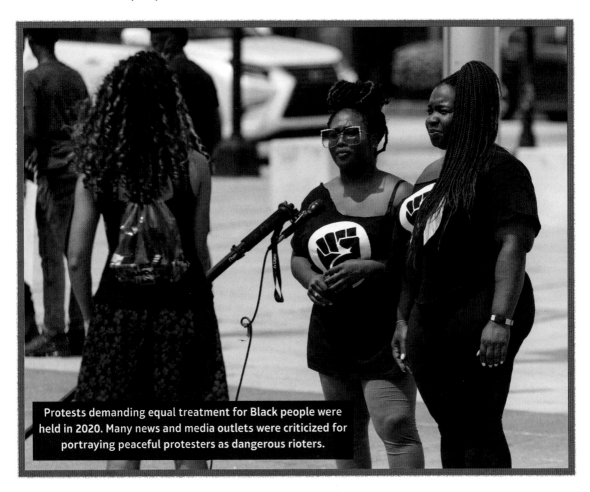

Protests demanding equal treatment for Black people were held in 2020. Many news and media outlets were criticized for portraying peaceful protesters as dangerous rioters.

Media organizations and audiences began to consider how they contributed to racial bias. They felt some media portrayed people of color in a harmful way. One example was a reality show called *Cops*. Starting in 1989, it recorded officers arresting people. Most of the officers on the show were white. Those arrested were often people of color. Critics said the show added to negative Black stereotypes. Some believed the show exploited people's worst moments. The show was canceled in 2020.

The Oprah Effect

Oprah Winfrey became the host of the local talk show *A.M. Chicago* in 1984. Within a year, the show went from the lowest-rated talk show to the highest. By 1986, Winfrey had her own nationwide talk show, *The Oprah Winfrey Show*. It remained on the air for twenty-five years and was the most-watched talk show in TV history. Winfrey fulfilled her dream of being an actress when she played Sofia in the 1985 film *The Color Purple*. She earned an Oscar nomination for the role and went on to act in several other movies. Winfrey is also a businesswoman. She owns the Harpo Productions television studio and runs *O: The Oprah Magazine*. She founded her own TV network called The Oprah Winfrey Network, or OWN. She became the first Black woman billionaire in 2003. She has donated millions of dollars to support education, which she often says is the door to freedom.

CELEBRATING BLACKNESS

Since 2010, creators have greatly expanded the range of Black stories in music, television, and film. These projects have not only challenged Black stereotypes. They have focused on celebrating Black history and stories.

In 2019, Beyoncé Knowles-Carter released the film *Homecoming*. It was a recording of the singer's 2018 performance at the Coachella music festival. The show featured art forms that began in historically Black colleges and universities. This included drumline performances and a dance style called stepping. Beyoncé wanted a large audience to witness the talent of young Black performers.

Beyoncé's 2020 visual album, *Black Is King*, highlights the customs of different African cultures, including clothing, hairstyles, music, and art. Beyonce said the film was meant to celebrate the beauty of Black ancestry. She wanted to make Black Americans feel proud of their history and heritage.

Beyoncé is one of the most celebrated Black artists of all time. She is the third-most honored female Grammy winner in history and the most-awarded artist at the Soul Train Awards, the BET Awards, and the MTV Video Music Awards.

? Creators are pushing for more diversity in media. What do you think we can gain from sharing more stories about different people and cultures?

MAJOR MOMENTS IN
Black Media

April 13, 1964: Sidney Poitier is the first Black man to win Best Actor at the Academy Awards.

1970–1979: Studios make more than 200 movies with mostly Black characters. Critics refer to the genre as Blaxploitation.

February 8, 1974: *Good Times* airs for the first time.

January 25, 1980: Robert L. Johnson launches the Black Entertainment Company (BET).

September 20, 1984: *The Cosby Show* debuts.

March 24, 2002: Halle Berry is the first Black woman to win Best Actress at the Academy Awards.

January 1, 2011: The Oprah Winfrey Network (OWN) debuts.

February 16, 2018: *Black Panther* is released. It is the first superhero movie with a mostly Black cast.

December 14, 2018: Miles Morales becomes the first Afro-Latino Spider-Man, in the animated film *Spider-Man: Into the Spider-Verse*.

July 31, 2020: *Black Is King* is released on Disney+.

Glossary

ancestry: a person's historical family background

blackface: makeup used to make someone look like a caricature of a Black person

Blaxploitation: the exaggerated use of Black people by movie producers in Black-oriented films

cultural appropriation: when a powerful culture adopts the styles, music, or other cultural markers of a less powerful culture, often without acknowledgment

enslaved: made into a slave; caused to lose freedom

exploited: used selfishly, such when work is taken without payment

heritage: what someone inherits, often used for what is passed down culturally

media: the television channels, radio stations, and newspapers that communicate news

minstrelsy: the practice of performing in a comedic way to ridicule ethnic or racial groups, often in blackface

police brutality: an act of violence, where police officers use excessive or unnecessary force on a citizen.

protagonist: the main character in a story

racial bias: usually negative attitudes, often unconscious, about another race

stereotypes: negative beliefs, often untrue, about certain groups of people

token minority: a person of a minority group who is hired or included to give the appearance of diversity, without being truly valued

Learn More

Godmother of Rock & Roll: Sister Rosetta Tharpe: PBS
https://www.pbs.org/black-culture/shows/list/rock-and-roll-rosetta-tharpe/

Kawa, Katie. *Chadwick Boseman is Black Panther.* New York: Gareth Stevens Publishing, 2020.

Miller, J. P. *Sister Rosetta Tharpe.* Vero Beach, FL: Rourke Educational Media, 2020.

Oprah Winfrey: Ducksters
https://www.ducksters.com/biography/entertainers/oprah_winfrey.php

Schwartz, Heather E. *Beyoncé: The Queen of Pop.* Minneapolis: Lerner Publications, 2019.

Why On-Screen Representation Matters, According to These Teens: PBS
https://www.pbs.org/newshour/arts/why-on-screen-representation-matters-according-to-these-teens

Index

Amos 'n' Andy, 15

Berry, Halle, 21, 29
Black Entertainment Television
(BET), 20, 21, 27, 28
Black Is King, 26, 29
Black Panther, 4, 5, 8, 29
Boseman, Chadwick, 5
Boyega, John, 9

Coachella, 26
The Cosby Show, 19, 20, 21, 28

DuVernay, Ava, 22

Floyd, George, 24

Good Times, 18, 20, 21, 28

Johnson, Robert L., 20, 28

Knowles-Carter, Beyoncé, 26, 27

Morales, Miles, 7, 8, 29

National Association for the
Advancement of Colored People
(NAACP), 16

Perry, Tyler, 22, 23
Poitier, Sidney, 21, 28

Sami, 19
Super Fly, 16, 17

T'Challa, 4, 8
Tharpe, Sister Rosetta, 13

Winfrey, Oprah, 25, 29

Photo Acknowledgments

The images in this book are used with the permission of: Alberto E. Rodriguez/
Getty Images, p.5; Anton_Ivanov/Shutterstock, p.6; Kevork Djansezian/Getty
Images, p.7; Sarah Morris/Getty Images, p.8; James Smith/Featureflash Photo
Agency/Shutterstock, p.9; Hulton Archive/Getty Images, p.11; John Pratt/Hulton
Archive/Getty Images, p.12; James Kriegsmann/Michael Ochs Archives/Getty
Images, p.13; Sasha/Getty Images, p.14; FPG/Archive Photos/Getty Images,
p.15; Michael Ochs Archives/Moviepix/Getty Images, p.17; Granamour Weems
Collection /Alamy Stock Photo, p.18; Tatiana Sall/iStock / Getty Images Plus/
Getty Images, p.19; Vince Bucci/Getty Images, p.20; Frederick M. Brown/Getty
Images, p.21; Kevin Winter/Getty Images, p.23; fitzcrittle/Shutterstock, p.24;
Steve Jennings/Getty Images, p.25; Kevin Winter/Coachella/Getty Images, p.27;
roseikeystrokes/Pixabay, background

Cover: Friedman-Abeles/Wikimedia, left; Frank Micelotta/Parkwood
Entertainment/Getty Images, middle; Faiz Zaki/Shutterstock, right